Copyright 2020 by Emily Yi -All rights reserved.

No part of this book may be reproduced or transmitted in any form or by any means, electronic or mechanical, including photocopying and recording, or by any information storage and retrieval system, without permission in writing from the publisher. This is a work of fiction. Names, places, characters and incidents are either the product of the author's imagination or are used fictitiously, and any resemblance to any actual persons, living or dead, organizations, events or locales is entirely coincidental. The unauthorized reproduction or distribution of this copyrighted work is ilegal.

Disclaimer Notice:

Please note the information contained within this document is for educational and entertainment purposes only. All effort has been executed to present accurate, up to date, reliable, complete information. No warranties of any kind are declared or implied. Readers acknowledge that the author is not engaged in the rendering of legal, financial, medical, or professional advice. The content within this book has been derived from various sources. Please consult a licensed professional before attempting any techniques outlined in this book.

By reading this document, the reader agrees that under no circumstances is the author responsible for any losses, direct or indirect, that are incurred as a result of the use of the information contained within this document, including, but not limited to, errors, omissions, or inaccuracies.

CONTENTS

- Introduction 4
- Appetizers 5
  - Mini Crab Cakes 5
  - Avocado Egg Rolls 6
  - Sweet Corn Cakes 7
  - Fried Mac and Cheese Balls 8
  - Honey Brown Bread 9
  - Warm Crab and Artichoke Dip 10
  - Buffalo Blasts 11
  - Tex-Mex Egg Rolls 12
  - Cheesecake Factory's Chicken Pot Stickers 13
  - Raspberry Lemonade 14
- Chicken 15
  - Chicken Madeira 15
  - Bang Bang Chicken and Shrimp 16
  - Chicken Piccata 17
  - Orange Chicken 18
  - Southern Fried Chicken Sliders 19
  - Chicken Costoletta 20
  - Chicken Romano 21
  - Louisiana Chicken Pasta 22
  - Barbecue Ranch Chicken Salad 23
  - Pasta Da Vinci 24
  - White Chicken Chili 25
  - Farfalle with Chicken and Roasted Garlic 26
  - Luau Salad 27
- Fish and Seafood 28
  - Cajun Jambalaya Pasta 28
  - Miso Glazed Salmon 29
  - Almond Crusted Salmon Salad 30
  - Shrimp Scampi 31
  - Bistro Shrimp Pasta 32
  - Crispy Crab Wontons 33
- Vegetarian 34
  - Tomato Basil Pasta 34
  - Evelyn's Favorite Pasta 35
  - Eggplant Parmesan 36
  - Four Cheese Pasta 37
  - Flatbread Pizza 38
- Beef and Pork 39
  - Shepherd's Pie 39
  - Meatloaf 40
  - Steak Diane 41
  - Pasta Carbonara 42
  - Grilled Steak Medallions 43
  - Cuban Sandwich 44
- Desserts 45
  - Pumpkin Cheesecake 45
  - Reese's Peanut Butter Chocolate Cake Cheesecake 46
  - White Chocolate Raspberry Swirl Cheesecake 48

Introduction

The Cheesecake Factory is a definite favorite dining choice for many people who are lucky enough to have one nearby. However, some people are not so fortunate. Here you will find some of the Cheesecake Factory's most popular and well-loved dishes. With these copycat recipes, you can have a taste of the restaurant's best dishes in the comfort of your own home. This compilation consists of recipes that are tributes to the originals, and yet distinctively their own.

In the 1940s, Evelyn Overton started making cheesecake, and everyone loved it so much that she started selling it. When her children came along she had to move her small production into her own home, but she continued baking and providing to some local restaurants.

Thirty years later, Evelyn and her husband moved to California. There, they started up Evelyn's business again, and with hard work, they built it up again. Soon Evelyn was offering an extensive menu with over 20 cheesecake flavors and other desserts.

The Cheesecake Factory as we know it now was founded in 1978, in Beverly Hills, California, by Evelyn's son, David. David's first menu was a single page, but it had 10 varieties of cheesecake. The Cheesecake Factory has an extensive menu. That is a well-known fact! With over 250 items on its menu, it offers something for everyone and the company prides itself on offering only the best quality ingredients and the freshest.

Under David's skilled management the restaurant grew into a chain. They changed the menu twice a year, adding new options – and always serving generous portions. In 1993 they went public, and as of summer 2018, there were 198 Cheesecake Factory restaurants, as well as a few related restaurants operating under other names, like Grand Lux Café and RockSugar Southeast Asian Kitchens. It is a very successful chain, now familiar in countries all over the world.

In this cookbook, you will find our favorite and classic Cheesecake Factory recipes to make at home. So let's get started and prepare a feast our friends and family will remember.

Carrot Cake Cheesecake 49
Original Cheesecake 50
Ultimate Red Velvet Cheesecake 51
Strawberry Shortcake 53
Lemoncello Cream Torte 54
Oreo Cookie Cheesecake 55
Banana Cream Cheesecake 56
Blackout Cake 57

Appetizers
Mini Crab Cakes

These mini crab cakes are one of Cheesecake Factory's bestselling appetizers. This take on the original recipe allows you to enjoy this seafood classic at home.

Makes 4 cakes | Prep. time 10 minutes | Cooking time 2–4 minutes

Ingredients

2 tablespoons mayonnaise
2 tablespoons green onion, minced (green part only)
2 tablespoons red bell pepper, minced
½ beaten egg
1 teaspoon fresh parsley, minced
1 teaspoon Old Bay seasoning
½ teaspoon prepared yellow mustard
½ pound lump crab meat
3 tablespoons plain breadcrumbs
¼ cup panko breadcrumbs
vegetable oil

Remoulade Sauce:
½ cup mayonnaise
2 teaspoons capers
2 teaspoons dill pickle slices, chopped
1 teaspoon lemon juice
½ teaspoon fresh parsley, minced
½ teaspoon paprika
½ teaspoon chili powder
¼ teaspoon cayenne pepper
¼ teaspoon ground cumin
⅛ teaspoon salt

Directions

1. In a large bowl, combine the mayo, green onions, red pepper, egg, parsley, Old Bay, mustard, crab meat, and the plain bread crumbs.
2. Gently mix the ingredients together. Don't over mix or the crab meat will fall apart too much.
3. Working carefully, form the mixture into 4 equal-sized flat patties.
4. Cover the patties with parchment paper and refrigerate for a couple of hours. Refrigerating will help the patty to set.
5. In the meantime, mix all of the ingredients for the Remoulade sauce together, making sure it is well combined.
6. After the crab cakes have had a chance to chill, heat enough oil in a large skillet so that the crab cake has enough to sit in.
7. Pour the panko breadcrumbs in a shallow dish and dip each crab cake into the panko, then place it in the skillet and cook for 2 to 3 minutes on each side. Remove the crab cakes from the skillet and allow them to drain on a paper towel. Serve with the remoulade sauce.

Avocado Egg Rolls

This is one of the Cheesecake Factory's most popular appetizers, and for good reason. This recipe is a copy of the original but tastes just as amazing.

Makes 8 egg rolls | Prep. time 15 minutes | Cooking time 5 minutes

Ingredients
3 avocados, halved, peeled and seeded
1 Roma tomato, diced
¼ cup diced red onion
2 tablespoons chopped fresh cilantro leaves
Juice of 1 lime
Kosher salt and freshly ground black pepper, to taste
1 cup vegetable oil
8 egg roll wrappers

<u>Cilantro Dipping Sauce</u>
¾ cup fresh cilantro leaves, loosely packed
⅓ cup sour cream
1 jalapeño, seeded and deveined (optional)
2 tablespoons mayonnaise
1 clove garlic
Juice of 1 lime
Kosher salt and freshly ground black pepper, to taste

Directions
1. First, mix together all of the ingredients for the cilantro dipping sauce, and set it aside.
2. In a medium mixing bowl, mash the avocados up a bit with the back of a fork. Gently mix in the tomato, onion, cilantro, lime juice, salt, and pepper.
3. In a deep skillet or saucepan, heat the vegetable oil over medium to high heat.
4. Take your egg roll wrappers and fill each one with some of the avocado mixture. Fold the sides over, and then fold down the top and bottom. You can wet your fingers and dampen the wrapper to seal the seams.
5. When the oil is heated, add the egg rolls and fry until they turn a beautiful golden brown. Then remove them and place them on a paper towel to drain.
6. Serve with cilantro dipping sauce.

Sweet Corn Cakes

These delicious Sweet Corn Cakes make a wonderful appetizer to any meal. This take on the Cheesecake Factory's recipe will soon be a regular in your rotation.

Serves 4 | Prep. time 15 minutes | Cooking time 15 minutes

Ingredients

For the Salsa Verde:
- 2 tomatillos, roughly chopped
- 1 (4-ounce) can diced green chilies, drained
- 1 green onion, sliced thin
- 2 tablespoons fresh cilantro, roughly chopped

For the Pico De Gallo:
- 1 large Roma tomato, diced
- 1 tablespoon red onion, diced
- 1 tablespoon fresh cilantro, minced

For Southwestern Sauce:
- ½ cup mayonnaise
- 1 teaspoon white vinegar
- 1 teaspoon water
- ½ teaspoon granulated sugar
- ½ teaspoon chili powder
- 1 ½ teaspoons granulated sugar
- ¼ teaspoon ground cumin
- ¼ teaspoon salt
- ⅛ teaspoon ground black pepper
- ½ teaspoon lime juice
- Salt and ground pepper to taste
- ¼ teaspoon paprika
- ⅛ teaspoon cayenne pepper
- ¼ teaspoon onion powder
- ⅛ teaspoon garlic powder

For the Corn Cakes:
- 1 ½ cups frozen sweet corn, divided
- ½ cup butter, softened to room temperature
- 3 tablespoons sugar
- ⅛ teaspoon salt
- ½ cup corn masa harina flour
- 2 tablespoons all-purpose flour
- 1 ½ tablespoons olive oil

For Garnish:
- Sour cream
- Avocado, diced
- Fresh cilantro, chopped

Directions

1. First, make the Salsa Verde. Pulse the ingredients for the Salsa Verde in the blender so it is roughly combined.
2. Make the Pico de Gallo and Southwestern Sauce by combining the ingredients together. When they are all well combined, cover them and put them in the refrigerator.
3. Prepare the corn cakes. First, place 1 cup of corn in the blender or food processor and purée.
4. Combine the puréed corn, butter, sugar, and salt in a medium bowl, and mix to combine.
5. In a small bowl, combine the masa and flour and stir.
6. Add the remaining corn and masa mixture to the butter and corn mixture and combine well, then form into patties.
7. Heat the oil in a large skillet over medium-low to medium heat. When oil is hot, add the corn cakes and fry on each side for about 5 to 8 minutes.
8. Serve with the salsa Verde, Pico de Gallo and Southwestern sauce for dipping. Garnish with sour cream, avocado, and cilantro.

Fried Mac and Cheese Balls

Macaroni and Cheese is an American favorite. Leave it to the Cheesecake Factory to take this classic and make it better. This copycat recipe pays homage to the Cheesecake Factory's wonderful recipe.

Serves 4-6 | Prep. time 15 minutes plus 3 hours chilling time | Cooking time 15 minutes

Ingredients

Sauce:
- 1 ¾ cups marinara sauce
- 1 ¾ cups alfredo sauce
- ¼ cup heavy whipping cream
- 1 teaspoon garlic powder
- ½ cup ricotta cheese
- 1 cup Italian blend shredded cheese
- ¼ cup red wine

Balls:
- 16 ounces grated white sharp cheddar, grated
- 16 ounces smoked gouda cheese, grated
- 3 tablespoons butter
- 2 tablespoons flour
- 2 cups whole milk, warmed
- 1 pound large elbow macaroni, cooked
- Salt and pepper, to taste
- 3 eggs
- 3 tablespoons milk
- 3 cups panko bread crumbs
- Fresh Parmesan cheese for garnish only
- vegetable oil for frying

Directions

1. Make the balls. In a mixing bowl, combine the shredded cheddar and shredded gouda.
2. In a large saucepan, melt the butter. Add the flour slowly, whisking until there are no lumps. Gradually add the 2 cups of warm milk. Whisk until smooth, and continue cooking until the sauce begins to thicken.
3. When the sauce is thickened, remove it from the heat and gradually mix in the cheddar and gouda cheeses. Stir until the cheese is melted and incorporated thoroughly.
4. Add the cooked macaroni and salt and pepper into the cheese sauce and stir well.
5. Butter a large cake pan and spread the mac and cheese mixture evenly into the pan, then place it in the refrigerator for at least two hours. You want the mixture to set and make it easier to form into balls.
6. After two hours, remove the tray from the refrigerator and form the mac and cheese into evenly sized balls about 2 inches in diameter. Cover, and put them in the freezer for at least an hour.
7. In a small bowl, beat your eggs and 3 tablespoons of milk together.
8. Place the bread crumbs in a shallow dish.
9. In a deep skillet or large saucepan, heat enough vegetable oil so that the balls will be covered when you fry them.
10. When the oil is heated to 350°F, dip each ball in the egg mixture, then the panko crumbs, and drop them into oil. Work in batches, and cook until the balls are a nice golden brown color, about 3–4 minutes. Transfer to paper towel as they finish cooking to drain.
11. Make your cheese sauce by combining the marinara and alfredo sauce in a small saucepan. Heat over medium and when warm, add the ricotta, Italian cheese blend, and wine. Stir to combine.
12. When the cheeses have melted, remove the pot from the heat and add the garlic powder and heavy cream. Stir well.
13. Serve the macaroni balls with the cheese sauce and a sprinkle of Parmesan.

Honey Brown Bread

This delicious brown bread is a Cheesecake Factory staple. This is a take on their amazing recipe.

6 mini-loaves | *Prep. time 30 minutes | Cooking time 30 minutes | Rising time 3–4 hours*

Ingredients
1 ½ cups warm water (105ºF)
1 tablespoon sugar
2 ¼ teaspoons instant dry yeast (1 package)
2 cups bread flour
1 ¾ cups whole wheat flour
1 tablespoon cocoa powder
2 teaspoons espresso powder (or instant coffee)
1 teaspoon salt
2 tablespoons butter, softened
¼ cup honey
2 tablespoons molasses
Caramel coloring, or dark brown food coloring (optional)
¼ cup cornmeal, for dusting the bottom of the shaped (not baked) loafs (optional)
Oats, for dusting the top of the shaped (not baked) loafs (optional)

Directions
1. Mix together the warm water, sugar, and yeast, and set aside for five minutes.
2. If you have a stand mixer, it is easiest to use that or a bread machine to mix your dough. With the whisk attachment on the stand mixer, mix together the flours, cocoa powder, espresso powder (or finely ground instant coffee), and the salt.
3. Add the yeast mixture you set aside as well as the butter, honey, and molasses. You can also add the food coloring if you choose to use it. At this point, you will need to switch to your dough hook attachment and let the mixer run on a medium speed until a dough is formed. This may take as long as 10 minutes.
4. Lightly oil a large bowl and transfer the dough to the bowl. Cover with a towel and place in a warm spot for two hours. It should double in size.
5. After it has doubled, divide the dough into 6 pieces and form them into loaves. Place the cornmeal in a shallow dish and place each loaf in the cornmeal and then move to a lined baking sheet. Make sure you leave enough room between the loaves for them to expand. Sprinkle the loaves with some oats if you would like. Then spray a little bit of cooking spray on each loaf before covering them loosely with plastic wrap and then allow them to rise again for about an hour or an hour and a half.
6. Preheat the oven to 350°F.
7. After the loaves have doubled in size, remove the plastic wrap and transfer the pan to the oven.
8. Bake 25–35 minutes, then remove from the oven and let sit for about 10–15 minutes before slicing and serving.

Warm Crab and Artichoke Dip

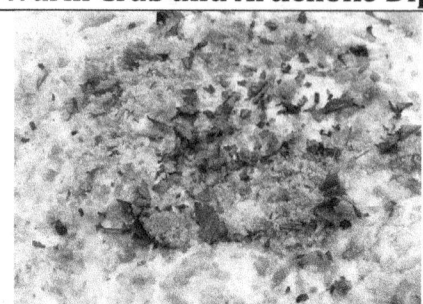

Serves 4 | Prep. time 10 minutes | Cook time 15 minutes

Ingredients
1 slice white bread, minced
3 ounces cream cheese
1 cup heavy cream
5 ounces sour cream
¼ cup mayonnaise
¼ teaspoon cayenne pepper
½ teaspoon kosher salt
¼ teaspoon ground black pepper
¼ teaspoon Old Bay Seasoning
6 ounces artichoke hearts, drained, cut into ¾-inch pieces
½ pound crab cake mix
¼ pound crab meat (lump or backfin)
Sourdough baguette, sliced in ½-inch pieces

Directions
1. In a mixing bowl, combine the minced bread and the cream cheese.
2. Pour the heavy cream over the bread and cream cheese mixture, and mix until everything is well combined
3. Into the bread mixture add the sour cream, mayonnaise, cayenne pepper, salt and pepper, and Old Bay seasoning and mix together.
4. Next, to the same bowl, add the artichoke hearts and crab cake mix and mix well.
5. Gently fold the crab into the mixture. Be careful that you don't mix too much, or the crab will shred completely; you'd like to have a few bigger pieces.
6. Transfer your crab mixture into a saucepan and heat over medium heat until hot and bubbly then transfer to a serving bowl.
7. Toast your slices of baguette and serve with the dip.

Buffalo Blasts

We have a love affair with all things "buffalo." Either wings or these fantastic blasts of flavor that the Cheesecake Factory created for their appetizer menu. This recipe is based on of the Cheesecake Factory original.

Serves 4-6 | Prep. time 5 minutes |

Ingredients
1 rotisserie chicken, shredded
¼ cup buffalo wing sauce
½ cup mozzarella cheese, shredded
1 cup oil for frying, pan plus extra if needed
24 wonton wrappers
2 large eggs lightly beaten with 1 tablespoon cold water
1 ½ cups Italian seasoned breadcrumbs
Oil to fry
Celery sticks for serving
Buffalo wing sauce and/or blue cheese dressing for serving

Directions
1. Mix together chicken, wing sauce, and cheese, stirring until well combined.
2. Heat the oil in a large skillet over medium-high heat.
3. Fill each wonton paper with some of the chicken mixture and moisten the seams to seal the wrapper. Seal up into a triangle shape.
4. Warm the oil in a deep skillet or using a deep fryer machine to 350^0F.
5. Brush each triangle with the egg mixture and dip into the breadcrumbs to coat on both sides. Fry in the oil for 2-3 minutes until golden brown and crispy. Fry in batches taking care of not overloading the pan or fryer. When cooked, place on a plate lined with kitchen towel to drain the excess fat.
6. Serve with celery sticks and your favorite dipping sauce like blue cheese or a Buffalo wing sauce.

Tex-Mex Egg Rolls

These crispy bites of Tex-Mex flavor are another Cheesecake Factory specialty. This recipe is inspired by those flavors created by the Cheesecake Factory chefs.

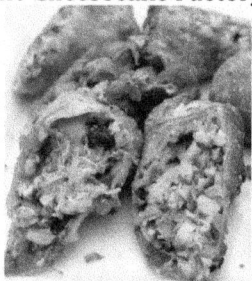

24 egg rolls | Prep. time 20 minutes | Cooking time 20 minutes

Ingredients

1 tablespoon canola oil
2 cups chicken breast, cooked and diced
½ yellow onion, diced
1 clove garlic, minced
1 teaspoon cumin
1 teaspoon chili powder
½ teaspoon kosher salt
1 cup black beans
1 cup corn
1 green bell pepper diced
1 Roma tomato, diced finely and dried on paper towel
½ cup cheddar cheese, shredded
2 tablespoons cilantro, chopped
24 egg roll wrappers
Canola oil for frying
8 ounces cream cheese
¼ cup sour cream
1 bunch cilantro
½ avocado

Directions

1. In a large, deep skillet heat 1 tablespoon of oil. When it is hot, add the chicken, onion, garlic, cumin and chili powder. Add salt to taste.
2. Cook for a couple of minutes or until the onion is soft and the garlic is fragrant. Then remove the pan from the heat and add the beans, corn, pepper, diced tomato, cheese, and cilantro. Stir well to combine. Transfer mixture to a bowl.
3. In your skillet, add enough oil to fry the egg rolls. About an inch or so.
4. Add enough mixture to each egg roll wrapper so that it is full, but not so full that you can't close up the seams.
5. Fold up the ends of the egg roll and tuck in the sides. Wet the ends of the egg roll to seal the edges.
6. When you are done wrapping and the oil is hot, add the egg rolls to the oil and cook until you achieve that nice golden brown color.
8. Remove the egg rolls from the oil to a plate lined with paper towel, to absorb excess oil.
9. In a mixing bowl, combine the cream cheese, sour cream, cilantro, and avocado. Mix together to form the dip.
10. Serve egg rolls with dip.

Cheesecake Factory's Chicken Pot Stickers

This is a good recipe whether you have guests over or just want to have a little snack. These chicken pot stickers taste just like Cheesecake Factory's special dish.

Yields 48 – Preparation Time: 15 minutes – Cooking Time: 45 minutes

Ingredients
Filling
1 ½ pounds ground chicken
½ cup red bell pepper, finely chopped
½ cup green cabbage, shredded
⅓ cup chopped green onions
2 teaspoons chopped ginger root
1 teaspoon sesame oil
¼ teaspoon white pepper

Other ingredients
1 egg white
1 cup water
1 package (10-ounces) round wonton skins
4 cups chicken broth, divided
4 teaspoons reduced-sodium soy sauce, divided

Dipping sauce
1 cup chicken broth
¼ cup soy sauce

Garnish
Green onions or chive, finely chiseled
Nori thin strips (optional)

Preparation
1. To make the filling, mix the filling ingredients together, thoroughly incorporating each ingredient into the mixture.
2. Brush each of the wonton skins with water.
3. Place 1 tablespoon of the stuffing mixture at the center of the wonton skin and fold the wrapper over, creating 5 pleats on one side of the wrapper. Seal the mixture inside.
4. Repeat steps 2 and 3 until you are out of filling.
5. Grease a large pan and cook the pot stickers in batches over medium heat until they turn light brown. Do not overcrowd the pan.
6. Increase the heat to medium-high. Pour 1 cup of the chicken broth and 1 teaspoon of soy sauce over the cooking pot stickers. Cover the pan and let the mixture sit until all the liquid has evaporated. Transfer the pot stickers to a plate, and cover with foil to keep them warm.
7. Repeat steps 6 and 7 for the remaining pot stickers.
8. To make the dipping sauce, use the same pan. Add 1 cup of chicken broth and ¼ cup soy sauce and bring to a boil on high heat. Scrape the pan's bottom to release all bits of flavor. Reduce the heat to medium and let it simmer until the sauce has reduce by half, about 3–5 minutes.
9. To serve, divide the pot stickers between serving plates add some of the dipping sauce. Garnish with green onions or chives, and thin nori strips, if desired.

Raspberry Lemonade

Serves 8 | Prep. time 2 minutes | cook time 3 minutes

Ingredients
1 cup water
1 cup sugar
1 cup freshly squeezed lemon juice
1 ½ cups fresh or frozen raspberries
Extra sugar for the rim of your glass

Directions
1. In a small saucepan, heat the water and sugar until the sugar completely dissolves.
2. Meanwhile, purée the raspberries in a blender. Add the contents of the saucepan and the cup of lemon juice. (If it's too thick you can add extra water.)
3. Wet the rim of your glass and dip it into a bit of sugar to coat the rim before pouring the lemonade into the glass.
4. Serve.

Chicken
Chicken Madeira

This Chicken Madeira recipe is a spin-off of one of the Cheesecake Factory's most loved recipes.

Serves 8 | Prep. time 40 minutes | Cook time 40 minutes

Ingredients

Chicken:
4 chicken breasts
1 cup balsamic vinaigrette
2 tablespoons brown sugar
2 tablespoons olive oil
1 cup mozzarella cheese, shredded
fresh parsley (for garnish)

Sauce:
2 tablespoons butter
2 cups white mushrooms, sliced
2 cups beef stock
¼ cup balsamic vinaigrette
2 tablespoons brown sugar

Directions

1. Preheat the oven to 350°F.
2. Place each chicken breast in between two pieces of plastic wrap or parchment paper and pound until they are about ¼-inch thick.
3. In a plastic bag, combine the vinaigrette, brown sugar, and olive oil, then add in the pounded chicken breasts. Refrigerate and let them marinate for at least an hour (but longer would be better).
4. When they are done marinating, you can either brown the breasts in a hot skillet by cooking for 2 minutes on each side, or you can skip this step if you are in a hurry.
5. Place the chicken breasts in a baking pan and bake for 12–15 minutes. Because the breasts are pounded thin, they won't take long to cook.
6. In the skillet you used to brown the chicken breasts, melt the butter over medium heat. Add the sauce ingredients and cook until the sauce reduces to about half the original amount.
7. Change the setting on your oven to broil. Cover each chicken breast with mozzarella and cook until the cheese melts.
8. Serve with the pan sauce.

Bang Bang Chicken and Shrimp

This spicy Bang Bang Chicken and Shrimp is one of the Cheesecake Factory's most famous dishes. This recipe pays tribute to their delicious entrée.

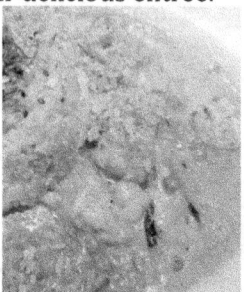

Serves 4 | Prep. time 20 minutes | Cooking time 40 minutes

Ingredients

Chicken and Shrimp
- 2 tablespoons vegetable oil
- 1 chicken breast, cut into bite-sized pieces
- ¼ cup cornstarch
- 10 medium shrimp, shelled

Peanut Sauce
- ¼ cup creamy peanut butter
- 2 tablespoons water
- 1 tablespoon sugar
- 1 tablespoon reduced sodium soy sauce
- 1 teaspoon rice vinegar
- 1 teaspoon lime juice
- ⅛ teaspoon red pepper flakes

Curry Coconut Sauce
- 1 teaspoon olive oil
- 1 teaspoon sesame oil
- ⅛ teaspoon red pepper flakes
- 2 cloves garlic, minced
- 1 small onion, chopped
- 1 teaspoon ginger, minced
- ½ cup water
- ½ teaspoon ground cumin
- ½ teaspoon ground coriander
- 1 teaspoon paprika
- ¼ teaspoon salt (or to taste)
- ¼ teaspoon pepper (or to taste)
- ¼ teaspoon allspice
- ¼ teaspoon turmeric
- 1 (14-ounce) can coconut milk
- 1 medium carrot, julienned
- 1 small zucchini, julienned
- ½ cup frozen peas

Garnish
- ½ cup flaked coconut, toasted
- ¼ cup peanuts, chopped
- 2 green onions, julienned or chopped
- Sesame seeds (optional)
- 2 cups rice, cooked

Directions

1. In a large skillet, heat the 2 tablespoons of oil. Salt and pepper the chicken pieces to taste and dip them into the corn starch. Do the same with the shrimp.
2. When the oil is hot, drop in the chicken and cook until it starts to brown, a couple of minutes or so. Then do the same with the shrimp, cooking the shrimp until it just starts to turn pink.
3. Place the chicken and shrimp on a plate and set them aside.
4. In a small saucepan, heat all of the ingredients for the peanut sauce. Cook until it just starts to boil, then remove it from the heat and set aside.
5. In another saucepan over medium heat, add 1 teaspoon of olive oil, sesame oil and crushed red pepper flakes. Add the garlic, chopped onion, and ginger, and cook just until the onion is soft. Add the water and all the spices for the curry sauce and stir to combine. Bring this mixture to a boil. When it starts to boil, add the coconut milk and return to a boil. Then reduce heat and allow to simmer for 20 minutes or until the sauce thickens nicely.
6. When the sauce has thickened, add the julienned carrots and zucchini, and stir in the peas last. Cook for about 10 more minutes, or until the carrots are tender.
7. To serve, place some rice on each plate and add some chicken and shrimp. Top with the curry sauce then add some of the peanut sauce on top of that. Garnish with any or all of the toppings listed above under garnish.

Chicken Piccata

There are Chicken Piccata recipes and then there is the Cheesecake Factory's recipe. This recipe is inspired by the Cheesecake Factory's and you will love being able to enjoy their amazing flavors at home.

Serves 4 | Prep. time 10 minutes | Cook time 15 minutes

Ingredients
2 tablespoons butter
2 tablespoons olive oi
4 boneless, skinless chicken breasts
Salt and pepper to taste
¼ cup all-purpose flour
6-8 white mushrooms, sliced thinly
1 cup chicken broth
2 whole lemons
¾ cup heavy cream
¼ cup capers
Chopped parsley, for garnish
1 pound angel hair pasta or any long similar pasta, cooked

Directions
1. In a large skillet, heat the butter and oil over medium-high heat.
2. If your chicken breasts are very thick, you may want to pound them down until they are about ¼ inch thick or so.
3. Season your chicken with salt and pepper to taste. Coat them with flour before adding them to the skillet.
4. Cook each breast for about 3 minutes on each side, until they are lightly browned and no longer pink. Remove them from the skillet, cover them with foil, and set them aside.
5. If needed, add more butter to the pan, add the mushrooms and stir-fry until golden around the edges, about 2-3 minutes.
6. Turn the heat down to medium low, and to the skillet add the chicken broth, the juice from the two lemons, the capers, and the heavy cream. Heat until it boils and reduce the heat and allow to simmer for about 3 more minutes.
7. To serve, plate some of the angel hair pasta, then top with a chicken breast and pour some sauce over the top. Garnish with parsley and fresh lemon slices.

Orange Chicken

The best thing about the Cheesecake Factory is its diverse menu. This recipe allows you to make your own version of their amazing orange chicken.

Serves 8 | Prep. time 5 minutes | Cooking time 30 minutes

Ingredients
Chicken:
1 ½ cups all-purpose flour
¼ teaspoon salt
¼ teaspoon pepper
1 egg
2 pounds boneless skinless chicken breasts, cut into 1 ½-inch cubes
Oil, for frying
Orange Sauce:
1 ½ cups water
2 tablespoons orange juice
¼ cup lemon juice
2 ½ tablespoons soy sauce
1 tablespoon grated orange peel
1 cup packed brown sugar
½ teaspoon minced ginger
½ teaspoon garlic powder
¼ teaspoon red pepper flakes
3 tablespoons cornstarch
2 tablespoons water
Rice for serving
Chopped parsley for garnish

Directions
1. In a shallow dish, mix together the flour, salt, and pepper. Beat the egg in another shallow dish. Dip the chicken pieces into the beaten egg first, then dredge them in the flour mixture.
2. In a large skillet, heat the oil over medium-high heat. When it is hot, add the chicken pieces and cook through. When thoroughly cooked, remove the chicken from the skillet and set it aside.
3. In a large saucepan, mix together the water, orange and lemon juice, and soy sauce. Heat over medium heat and when well combined and hot, add the orange peel, brown sugar, ginger, garlic powder, and red pepper flakes. Bring it to a boil.
4. In a small dish, make a slurry of the cornstarch and water. Whisking constantly, slowly add it to the saucepan to thicken the sauce.
5. To serve, pour the sauce over the chicken pieces. Serve with rice and a sprinkle of chopped parsley.

Southern Fried Chicken Sliders

These chicken sliders are a home version inspired by the Cheesecake Factory's popular dish. Serve as an appetizer for 6 or a main course for 4.

Makes 12 sliders | *Prep. time 15 minutes | Cooking time 10 minutes*

Ingredients
Vegetable oil for frying
1 cup bread crumbs
1 tablespoon garlic powder
2 teaspoons onion powder
1 teaspoon ground black pepper
1 teaspoon paprika
¼ teaspoon ground cayenne pepper
½ cup buttermilk
6 (6-ounce) boneless and skinless chicken breasts, cut in half to make 12 pieces

For serving
6 large lettuce leaves, cut in half to make 12 pieces
3 Roma tomatoes, sliced
2 large dill pickles, sliced
12 slider buns
Butter, at room temperature
Mayonnaise and or Thousand Island dressing for serving

Directions
1. Preheat the oil in a deep large skillet (should have about 1 ½ inch of oil in the pan) or you can use a deep fryer. Let the oil warm until it gets to 350°F.
2. In a shallow dish, combine the breadcrumbs, garlic powder, onion powder, pepper, paprika, and cayenne pepper. Stir with a fork to make sure the spices are thoroughly combined.
3. Pour the buttermilk in another shallow dish. Dip each piece of chicken into the buttermilk and then into the spice mixture.
4. Working in batches so to not crowed the pan or fryer, place chicken pieces carefully in the warm oil and fry until browned and cooked through, about 3-4 minutes per side. Turn over after 2 minutes.
5. When done, remove the chicken from the oil and place on a plate covered with paper towel to absorb excess fat. Set aside.
6. Start oven broiler, and place oven rack in the middle position. Separate buns in 2 and butter lightly each piece. Place buns on a baking sheet and broil until golden, about 1 minute.
7. Place a chicken piece on each bun bottom and add top bun. Serve 2 or 3 sliders per person. Add enough lettuce leaves, tomato slices and pickle slices to each plate. Serve with your favorite sauce such as mayonnaise or Thousand Island dressing.

Chicken Costoletta

This recipe is inspired by the Cheesecake Factory's popular menu item. Now you can enjoy one of your restaurant favorites at home.

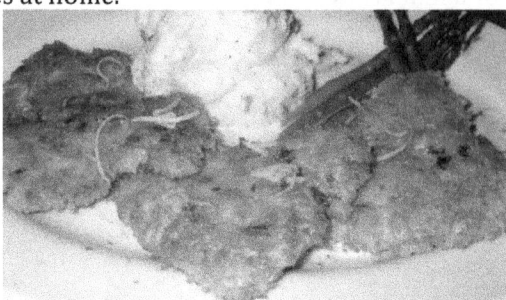

Serves 4 | Prep. time 20 minutes | Cooking time 20 minutes

Ingredients

For the Chicken
8 (2--ounce) chicken tenders
½ cup all-purpose flour
2 large eggs
1 cup panko breadcrumbs

For the Sauce
1 tablespoon extra-virgin olive oil
2 cloves garlic, minced
1 tablespoon all-purpose flour
¼ cup milk

For serving
Steamed green beans
Mashed potatoes
Orange zest

Zest of 1 lemon
¼ cup pecorino Romano cheese, grated
¼ cup extra-virgin olive oil
2 tablespoons butter

¾ cup heavy cream
¼ cup fat-free chicken stock
Juice of 1 lemon
1 tablespoon butter

Directions

1. Pound the chicken tenderloins until they are flat and approximately all the same thickness.
2. Place the flour in a shallow dish. In another shallow dish, beat the eggs. In a third dish, combine the panko breadcrumbs, lemon zest, and cheese.
3. Heat the olive oil and butter in a large skillet. When the oil is hot, take each piece of chicken and dip it first in the flour, then in the egg, then in the breadcrumb mixture. When coated, place the tenders in the hot skillet and cook until done, about 4–5 minutes on each side.
4. When the chicken is done, remove it from the skillet and set it on paper towel to drain.
5. Make the sauce. In a saucepan over medium heat, heat the olive oil. When it is hot, add the garlic and cook a minute or so then add in the flour and whisk until there are no lumps.
6. Whisk in the milk, cream, chicken stock, and lemon juice. Heat to a low boil, allowing the sauce to thicken.
7. When it is thick, add the butter and stir to combine.
8. Spoon some sauce on each plate, top with chicken. Serve with green beans and mashed potatoes. Sprinkle with orange zest..

Chicken Romano

This recipe is another one inspired by the Cheesecake Factory's classic favorites. Bring the Cheesecake Factory tastes to your own kitchen.

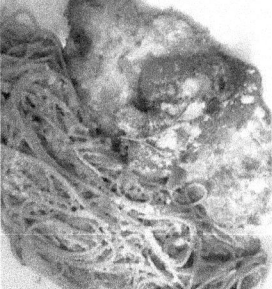

Serves 4–6 | Prep. time 5 minutes | Cooking time 10 minutes

Ingredients
2 eggs
1 cup breadcrumbs
1 cup Romano cheese, shredded
3 boneless skinless chicken breasts
Salt and pepper to taste
All-purpose flour
¼ cup butter
Juice of 1 lemon
1 (16-ounce) can of tomato sauce
¼ cup heavy cream
Cooked spaghetti noodles
Parmesan cheese

Directions
1. In a shallow dish, beat the eggs. In a second shallow dish, combine the breadcrumbs and the cheese and mix well.
2. Cut the chicken breasts in half and pound each half to approximately ¼-inch thickness.
3. Sprinkle each piece of chicken with salt and pepper, then dust the chicken with some flour. Dip each floured piece into the eggs and then into the breadcrumbs.
4. In a large skillet, melt the butter. When it is hot, add the chicken and cook for about 5–6 minutes on each side, until the pieces are a light golden brown. When cooked through, remove them from the heat and squeeze a bit of lemon juice over each piece.
5. In a small saucepan, heat the tomato sauce. When it is warm, whisk in the heavy cream.
6. Serve the chicken on the pasta with sauce over the top, and a sprinkle of Parmesan cheese.

Louisiana Chicken Pasta

This recipe is a variation of the Cheesecake Factory's famous Louisiana Chicken Pasta. The crunch of the chicken and the heat of the Cajun seasoning makes this dish an absolute favorite.

Serves 4 | Prep. time 15 minutes | Cook time 15 minutes

Ingredients

Cajun Cream Sauce:
- 1 teaspoon red pepper flakes
- 1 teaspoon Cajun seasoning
- ½ teaspoon kosher salt
- ¼ teaspoon ground black pepper
- 2 cups heavy cream
- 1 cup chicken stock
- 1 tablespoon cornstarch
- 1 cup Parmesan cheese, shredded

Vegetables:
- 2 tablespoons butter
- ½ yellow bell pepper, sliced
- ½ red bell pepper, sliced
- ½ red onion, sliced
- 1 tablespoon garlic, minced
- 8 ounces cremini mushrooms, sliced

Crispy Parmesan Chicken:
- ¼ cup all-purpose flour
- 1 cup breadcrumbs
- ½ cup Parmesan cheese, grated
- ½ teaspoon kosher salt
- ¼ teaspoon ground black pepper
- 2 eggs
- 4 chicken breasts, butterflied
- ¼ cup vegetable oil

Other ingredients
- 1 pound Farfalle pasta, cooked al dente
- ¼ cup parsley for garnish (optional)

Directions

1. In a mixing bowl, combine all of the ingredients for the Cajun cream sauce, and set it aside.
2. Prepare the vegetables. Heat 2 tablespoons of butter in a large skillet. When it is melted, add the peppers, onion, garlic and the mushrooms and cook 3–5 minutes, then remove them from the pan.
3. Make the chicken. In a shallow dish, mix together the flour, breadcrumbs, Parmesan cheese, salt, and pepper.
4. In another shallow dish beat the 2 eggs.
5. Place each piece of chicken into the flour mixture, then the egg, then the flour again.
6. In the same skillet used for the vegetables, warm the ¼ cup of oil over medium-high heat. When hot, add the coated chicken and cook 4–5 minutes on each side, or until the chicken is golden brown and crispy. Remove the chicken from the skillet and set it aside.
7. Drain the excess oil out of the skillet and add the cooked pasta, vegetables, and sauce mixture into the pan. Cook for about 5 minutes, or until the sauce starts to thicken.
8. Serve the pasta and sauce with chicken on top.

Barbecue Ranch Chicken Salad

The Cheesecake Factory has super flavorful salads; this recipe is inspired by their Barbecue Ranch Chicken Salad.

Serves 4 | Prep. time 5 minutes | Cooking time 25 minutes

Ingredients
BBQ Ranch Dressing:
¾ cup mayonnaise
½ cup buttermilk
¼ cup barbecue sauce (your choice)
1 tablespoon Hidden Valley Ranch® powder
1 small garlic clove, grated
Cracked black pepper, to taste
4 chicken breasts
1 cup barbecue sauce (your choice), divided
Salt and pepper, to taste
3–4 heads Romaine lettuce, chopped
2 tomatoes, diced
2 ears corn, shucked, rinsed and kernels cut from the cob
1 can black beans, rinsed and drained
1 avocado, diced
Fresh cilantro, chopped (optional)
Bag of crisp fried onions

Directions
1. Mix all the ingredients for the dressing together in a mixing bowl.
2. Cut the chicken breasts into bite-sized pieces, and season them with salt and pepper. (You can either grill your chicken and cut it up after cooking, or fry it up and cut it before cooking. Either way, cook until completely done, basting with the barbecue sauce while cooking.
3. Next, assemble your salad. Top it with cooked chicken, crispy fried onions, and barbecue ranch dressing. Serve

Pasta Da Vinci

The kick in this pasta dish will wake up your taste buds. This is a variation of the Cheesecake Factory's popular dish.

Serves 4-6 | Prep. time 10 minutes | Cooking time 20 minutes

Ingredients

For the chicken:
1 tablespoon olive oil
1 pound chicken tenders or breasts cut in 1-inch cubes
Salt to taste

For the vegetables:
¼ cup butter
1 red onion, chopped
8 ounces mushrooms, sliced

Wine Sauce:
2 tablespoons butter
4 cloves garlic, chopped
1 tablespoon all-purpose flour
1 cup Madeira wine (sherry or marsala will also work)
½ cup heavy cream
½ cup chicken stock
½ cup Parmesan cheese
Salt and pepper to taste
⅛ teaspoon red pepper flakes

Pasta:
1 pound any tubular pasta (such as penne or rigatoni), cooked

Directions

1. In a skillet, heat the olive oil. When it is hot, add the chicken cubes and cook until browned and cooked through. Remove them from the skillet and set them aside.
2. Add the butter to the skillet and turn the heat to medium high. Add the onion and cook until translucent.
3. Stir in the mushrooms and cook until soft, then remove the vegetables from the skillet.
4. Make the wine sauce: melt 2 tablespoons of butter in the skillet, add the garlic, and cook until fragrant (about 1 minute). Whisk in the flour and cook for about 1 minute.
5. Reduce the heat and stir in the wine, whisking out any lumps. Bring it to a light boil. Add the cream and the chicken stock, stirring until well combined, and cooking for about 5 minutes. Remove the skillet from the heat and add the Parmesan cheese, salt and pepper, and red pepper flakes.
6. Add the mushrooms and onions back to the skillet and stir to combine. Cook for about 1 minute, then add the chicken.
7. Finally, add the pasta to the skillet mixture. Heat through, and serve.

White Chicken Chili

The Cheesecake Factory's White Chicken Chili is one of their most popular dishes. This recipe allows you to make this spicy dish at home.

Serves 4 | Prep. time 5 minutes | Cooking time 1 hour

Ingredients

- ¼ cup canola oil
- 2 pounds chicken breasts, cut into ¾-inch pieces
- 1 ½ teaspoons cumin, ground
- 1 ½ teaspoons chili powder
- 1 ½ teaspoons kosher salt
- ¾ teaspoon ground black pepper
- 2 tablespoons butter
- 2 tablespoons canola oil
- ¾ cup yellow onion, diced
- 1 tablespoon garlic, minced
- ½ cup green poblano chilies, roasted, peeled, seeds removed, diced
- ½ cup all-purpose flour
- 1 quart chicken stock
- 2 tablespoons salsa verde
- 1 ½ teaspoons chili garlic sauce
- 1 ½ teaspoons hot sauce
- ¾ teaspoon oregano, dried
- ¾ teaspoon brown sugar
- ¼ teaspoon cumin, ground
- 2 cups canned white beans, rinsed and drained
- 3 tablespoons sour cream
- 2 cups white rice, cooked
- ¼ cup pico de gallo or salsa
- ¼ cup green onions, chopped

Directions

1. In a large saucepan, heat the canola oil over medium-high heat.
2. In a mixing bowl, combine chicken with the cumin, chili powder, salt, and pepper.
3. When the oil is hot, add the chicken and cook until it is almost done but not quite. Remove it from the saucepan and set it aside.
4. Heat the 2 tablespoons of butter and 2 tablespoons of oil in the same saucepan you cooked the chicken in. Add the onion and cook until soft, then add the minced garlic and chilies and stir to combine.
5. After about 30 seconds, whisk in the flour and cook an additional 2 minutes, then whisk in the chicken stock, stirring until there are no lumps. Cook another 2 minutes.
6. Next, add the salsa verde, chili sauce, hot sauce, oregano, brown sugar, and cumin. Bring the mixture back to a simmer. When it simmers, add the chicken to the pot and cook for about 5 minutes.
7. Stir in the sour cream and beans. When the beans are hot, serve with white rice and garnish with pico de gallo or salsa and green onions.

Farfalle with Chicken and Roasted Garlic

This rich creamy pasta is another dish the Cheesecake Factory is famous for. This recipe is inspired by their delicious entrée.

Serves 4 | Prep. time 15 minutes | Cook time 35 minutes

Ingredients
2 boneless skinless chicken breasts
½ teaspoon kosher salt
¼ teaspoon coarse ground black pepper
2 tablespoons extra-virgin olive oil
12 ounces center-cut bacon, cut into strips
8 ounces cremini mushrooms quartered
½ yellow onion, chopped
½ cup sundried tomatoes, roughly chopped (reserve the oil)
¾ cup white wine
1 cup heavy cream
1 head roasted garlic
¾ cup Parmesan cheese, divided
1 pound bow tie pasta (farfalle), cooked and drained (but not rinsed)

Directions
1. Cube the chicken and season it with salt and black pepper.
2. In a large skillet, warm the olive oil over high heat.
3. Cook the chicken until lightly browned on both sides, about 6 minutes. When it is browned, remove it from the skillet and set it aside. Add the bacon to the skillet and cook until crisp.
4. When the bacon is done, stir in the mushrooms and onion and cook for about 5 minutes, or until soft, then remove them from the skillet.
5. Next, add the sundried tomatoes and white wine to the skillet. Stir and let it cook until the liquid reduces to half volume, about 12–15 minutes.
6. When reduced, stir in the heavy cream, roasted garlic, chicken, and vegetables.
7. Stir in most of the Parmesan cheese, saving a little for garnishing.
8. Stir in the pasta and serve with the remaining Parmesan cheese sprinkled on top.

Luau Salad

This crunchy salad is a variation of the recipe made famous at The Cheesecake Factory.

Serves 6 | Prep. time 35 minutes | Cooking time 10 minutes

Ingredients
3 chicken breasts, grilled and sliced into thin strips
½ teaspoon Chinese five spice powder
6 cups mixed greens
1 red bell pepper, thinly sliced
1 yellow bell pepper, thinly sliced
1 ½ cups fresh green beans, blanched and cut into 3-inch pieces
1 fresh mango, diced
1 red onion, diced
1 cup cucumber slices
Dressing
¼ cup seasoned rice vinegar
1 teaspoon sesame oil
¼ cup balsamic vinaigrette
¼ cup granulated sugar
1 teaspoon Kosher salt
¼ teaspoon ground black pepper
Toppings
¼ cup green onions, sliced into 1-inch thin strips
¼ cup sweet and sour sauce
¼ cup macadamia nuts, toasted and chopped
½ cup carrots, peeled and sliced into 1-inch thin strips
2 teaspoons white sesame seeds
2 teaspoons black sesame seeds
8 (6-inch) wonton wrappers, fried crisp

Directions
1. In a bowl, season the chicken with the five spice powder and toss it with the other salad ingredients: greens, peppers, beans, mango, onion, and cucumber.
2. In another small bowl, whisk together the seasoned rice vinegar, the balsamic vinaigrette, sesame oil and granulated sugar. Add salt and pepper to taste.
3. Toss the salad with the dressing, mixing well.
4. Lightly brush the crispy wontons with a bit of the sweet and sour sauce.
5. To serve, set out individual salad bowls or plates. Layer the salad mixture with the crispy wontons, and then top with whichever of the toppings you choose.

Fish and Seafood
Cajun Jambalaya Pasta

This spicy pasta recipe is a tribute to the Cheesecake Factory's Cajun Jambalaya. You will love making this rich dish at home.

Serves 6 | Prep. time 10 minutes | Cook Time 50 minutes

Ingredients

- ¼ cup unsalted butter
- ¼ cup extra-virgin olive oil
- 1 pound andouille sausage or smoked sausage, sliced
- 1 pound boneless skinless chicken breast, cubed
- 1 bell pepper, diced
- 1 white onion, diced
- 3 stalks celery, diced
- 4 cloves garlic, minced
- 1 pound jumbo shrimp, peeled and deveined
- 2 cups red salsa
- 1 (6-ounce) can hot tomato sauce
- 1 quart low-sodium chicken broth
- 1 bay leaf
- ¼ cup Italian parsley, chopped
- ½ bunch green onions
- 1 pound linguine pasta, cooked according to the package directions

Spice Blend
- 1 tablespoon creole seasoning
- 1 tablespoon garlic powder
- 1 tablespoon onion powder
- 2 teaspoons black pepper
- 1 teaspoon paprika
- Pinch cayenne pepper
- Garlic bread, for serving

Directions

1. In a small dish, mix together all the spices for the spice blend.
2. Season the chicken chunks with 1 tablespoon of the spice blend. Mix until the chicken is well coated, and set it aside.
3. In a large saucepan, melt the butter and heat olive oil over medium heat.
4. When it is hot, add the sausage slices and cook for 5 minutes. Add the chicken and cook for about 10 minutes.
5. Next, add the bell pepper, onion, and celery. Mix in half of the remaining spice blend. Cook for approximately 10 minutes, then add the garlic and cook 1 more minute.
6. With 1 tablespoon of seasoning blend, season the shrimp and set it aside. Then add the rest of the spices to the saucepan and stir to combine.
7. Add the salsa, tomato sauce, chicken broth, and the bay leaf. Mix together and bring it to a boil, stirring it together so that everything is well combined. Don't forget to scrape the bottom of the pan for brown bits.
8. Reduce the heat and let it simmer, covered, for about 30 minutes. Once the 30 minutes is up, discard the bay leaf. Add the shrimp, parsley, and green onions, and cook, still covered for about 10 minutes more.
9. Serve over pasta with a slice of toasted garlic bread.

Miso Glazed Salmon

This light glazed salmon recipe is inspired by the Cheesecake Factory's menu favorite. Enjoy the Factory at home with this easy recipe.

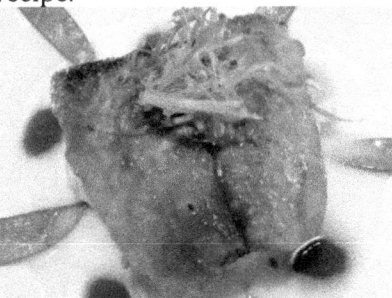

Serves 4 | Prep. time 10 minutes | Cook time 10 minutes

Ingredients
½ cup brown sugar
3 tablespoons soy sauce
¼ cup hot water
3 tablespoons miso (soybean paste)
4 salmon fillets
1 tablespoon butter
2 tablespoons ginger paste
1 tablespoon garlic paste
½ cup sake
1 tablespoon heavy cream
½ cup butter, cut into 8 pieces
Juice of half of a lime
For serving:
Steamed snow peas, broccoli, and carrots
Steamed Jasmine Rice

Directions
1. Preheat the broiler.
2. Mix together the brown sugar, soy sauce, hot water, and miso paste. Stir until well combined.
3. Lightly oil a baking dish and arrange the salmon fillets in it. Spoon some of the miso mixture over each fillet, leaving some for basting. Transfer the pan to the oven and broil for about 10 minutes. Baste every 3 minutes while broiling.
4. In the meantime, in a small saucepan, melt 1 tablespoon of butter over medium-high heat. Add the ginger and garlic paste, and cook for about 2 minutes.
5. Stir in the sake and bring the mixture to a boil. Let it cook for 3 more minutes, and add the heavy cream. Cook another 2 minutes, or until the sauce starts to reduce. Then whisk in the remaining butter one piece at a time and cook until the sauce thickens. Remove the saucepan from the heat and stir in the lime juice.
6. When the salmon is done, serve by pouring a little sauce over the rice and top with a salmon fillet with vegetables on the side.

Almond Crusted Salmon Salad

This copycat recipe is an easy way to bring a taste of the Cheesecake Factory to your own kitchen.

Serves 4 | Prep. time 15 minutes | Cooking time 30 minutes

Ingredients
¼ cup olive oil
4 (4-ounce) portions salmon
½ teaspoon kosher salt
⅛ teaspoon ground black pepper
2 tablespoons garlic aioli (bottled is fine)
½ cup chopped and ground almonds for crust
10 ounces kale, chopped
¼ cup lemon dressing of choice
2 avocados, peeled, pitted and cut into ½-inch pieces
2 cups cooked quinoa
1 cup brussels sprouts, sliced
2 ounces arugula
½ cup dried cranberries
1 cup balsamic vinaigrette
24 thin radish slices
Lemon zest

Directions
1. In a large skillet, heat the olive oil over medium-high heat. Sprinkle the salmon with salt and pepper to season. When the skillet is hot, add the fish fillets and cook for about 3 minutes on each side, or until it flakes easily with a fork. Top the salmon with garlic aioli and sprinkle with nuts.
2. Meanwhile, combine all the salad ingredients, including the quinoa, in a bowl and toss with the dressing.
3. Serve the salad with a fish fillet on top of greens and sprinkle with radishes and lemon zest.

Shrimp Scampi

Scampi is a classic and this recipe, inspired by the Cheesecake Factory's entrée, is sure to satisfy your cravings.

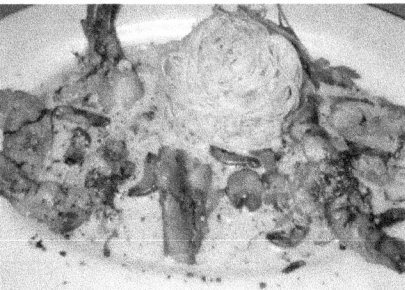

Serves 4 | Prep. time 10 minutes | Cooking time 30 minutes

Ingredients

- 1–2 pounds fresh shrimp, cleaned, deveined, and butterflied
- 1 cup milk
- 3 tablespoons olive oil
- ½ cup all-purpose flour
- 4 tablespoons Parmesan cheese, divided
- ¼ teaspoon salt
- ½ teaspoon fresh ground black pepper
- ¼ teaspoon cayenne pepper
- 6–8 whole garlic cloves
- 1 cup dry white wine
- 2 cups heavy cream
- 5–7 leaves fresh basil, cut into strips
- 1 diced tomato
- 2 tablespoons Parmesan cheese, finely grated
- 1 shallot, diced
- 1 pound angel hair pasta, cooked (hot)
- Parsley, to garnish

Directions

1. Put the shrimp in the milk and let it sit.
2. In a shallow bowl, combine the flour, 2 tablespoons of Parmesan, salt, pepper, and cayenne.
3. Pour the olive oil in a large skillet, making sure it's enough to cover the bottom. Heat over medium-high heat.
4. Take the shrimp from the milk and dredge in flour mixture. Transfer it to the skillet and cook about 2 minutes on each side. After the shrimp cooks, transfer it to a plate covered with a paper towel to drain.
5. Reduce the heat to medium-low and cook the garlic in the leftover oil. (Don't worry about any bits left from the shrimp because these will add flavor and help to thicken the sauce.)
6. After the garlic cooks for a couple of minutes, add the wine. Increase the heat and bring the mixture to a boil, then reduce the heat and simmer to reduce liquid to about half of the original volume.
7. Add the cream and simmer for about 10 more minutes, then add the basil, tomato, cheese, and shallots. Stir to combine.
8. Add the shrimp to the skillet and remove it from the heat.
9. Arrange the pasta on serving plates, topped with shrimp and covered with sauce. Garnish with parsley.

Bistro Shrimp Pasta

An all-time favorite dish from the Cheesecake Factory. This is a home version that takes its inspiration from the restaurant recipe.

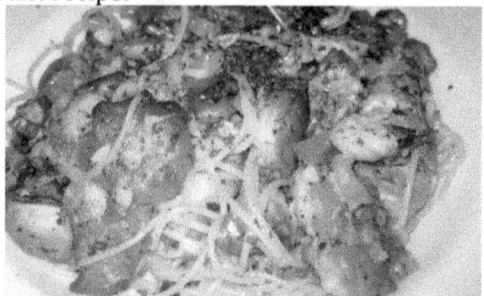

Serves 8 | Prep. time 30 minutes | Cooking time 45 minutes

Ingredients

2 tablespoons olive oil
1 cup button mushrooms, quartered
For the Lemon Basil Cream Sauce
¼ cup butter
4 garlic cloves, minced
2 cups heavy whipping cream
2 cups chicken broth
For the shrimp

1 cup grape tomatoes, halved
1 pound thin spaghetti, cooked

½ cup lemon juice
¼ cup cornstarch
½ teaspoon pepper
1 cup chopped fresh basil

1 pound raw shrimp, deveined and with shells removed
2 eggs, beaten
1 cup flour
1 cup panko
1 teaspoon garlic powder
1 teaspoon Italian seasoning
3 tablespoons butter

Directions

1. In a small skillet, cook the mushrooms in 2 tablespoons of olive oil. When they are soft, stir in the tomatoes and set the skillet aside.
2. Make the cream sauce: in a large skillet, melt the butter. Add the garlic and cook until fragrant. Pour in the cream and chicken broth, and bring to a low boil. Reduce the heat and let the sauce cook until the liquid reduces by half.
3. In a small dish, whisk the corn starch into the lemon juice, mixing until it is smooth and free of lumps, making a slurry. Add the slurry into the chicken broth mixture.
4. To make the shrimp, beat the eggs in one small dish and combine the panko, flour, garlic powder, and Italian seasoning in a different one. Then dip each shrimp in the egg mixture and then into the panko.
5. Using the skillet you cooked the mushroom and tomatoes in, melt the 3 tablespoons of butter. When the shrimp turns nicely golden, remove it from skillet and let it drain on a plated lined with paper towel.
6. Add the fresh basil to the sauce and stir.
7. To serve, put some pasta on the plate, cover with sauce, and top with shrimp.

Crispy Crab Wontons

This may be one of the Cheesecake Factory's best appetizers. This recipe lets you bring that home and add it to your table.

Serves 4 | Prep. time 10 minutes | Cooking time 15 minutes

Ingredients
4 ounces cream cheese
2 tablespoons sweet and sour chili sauce (plus more for serving)
1 ½ teaspoons mustard
1 teaspoon chili garlic paste
1 teaspoon lemon juice
½ teaspoon granulated sugar
4 ounces crab meat
2 ounces sliced water chestnuts, minced
2 tablespoons green onions, finely chopped
1 ounce mozzarella cheese, grated
1 ounce fontina cheese, grated
¼ cup panko breadcrumbs
25 small square wonton wrappers, approximately 3-½ inches
Oil for frying

Directions
1. In a large bowl, mix together the cream cheese, sweet and sour sauce, mustard, garlic paste, lemon juice, and sugar. Stir until well combined, then gently add in the crab, the water chestnuts, and green onions.
2. In a separate bowl, combine the mozzarella, fontina, and panko breadcrumbs. Carefully fold them into the cream cheese mixture, until well distributed.
3. Heat enough oil in a large skillet or saucepan so that the wontons won't touch the bottom when you cook them.
4. Lay out a wonton wrapper and fill it with about a teaspoon of filling. Pinch the sides of the wonton up and seal with a bit of water on your fingers.
5. When the oil is about 350°F, fry the wontons until they turn a golden brown. Transfer them to a plate lined with paper towel to drain.
6. Serve the wontons with sweet and sour chili sauce.

Vegetarian
Tomato Basil Pasta

Feel like a meat-free meal? This recipe is a copycat of the Cheesecake Factory's similar dish.

Serves 6 | Prep. time 15 minutes | Cooking time 1 hour

Ingredients
¼ cup plain Greek yogurt
⅓ cup light sour cream
¼ cup olive oil
3 cloves garlic, minced
⅓ cup sundried tomato halves, sliced
1 (14.5-ounce) can of petite diced tomatoes, drained
3 tablespoons tomato paste
½ tablespoon granulated sugar
2 cups baby spinach
Pinch of salt and pepper
8 ounces fettuccine, cooked

Directions:
1. In a mixing bowl, stir together the yogurt and the sour cream.
2. In a large skillet, heat the olive oil over medium-high heat. Add the garlic and cook for about 1 minute, then add the sundried tomatoes and cook for 2 minutes.
3. To the skillet add the diced tomatoes, tomato paste, and sugar. Cook for a couple of minutes, and then stir in the spinach, salt, and pepper.
4. Whisk the yogurt mixture into the tomato sauce.
5. To serve, plate some pasta and top with sauce.

Evelyn's Favorite Pasta

Another Cheesecake Factory favorite inspired this copycat recipe that will be sure to please.

Serves 4 | Prep. time 10 minutes | Cooking time 10 minutes

Ingredients
2 tablespoons olive oil
4 cloves garlic, sliced
1 cup eggplant, diced
1 cup broccoli florets
1 red pepper, deseeded and chopped
2 tablespoons sundried tomatoes, finely chopped
1 cup artichoke hearts, quartered
¼ cup Kalamata olives, pitted and sliced
¼ cup pine nuts
1 tablespoon fresh basil, minced
1 pound cavatappi pasta, cooked
Parmesan cheese, freshly grated, for garnish

Directions
1. Heat about 2 tablespoons of olive oil over medium heat in a large skillet. When the oil is hot, add in the garlic and cook until fragrant.
2. When the garlic is fragrant, add the eggplant, broccoli, red pepper, and sundried tomatoes and cook for about 8 minutes, or until the vegetables are cooked to your liking.
3. Next, stir in the artichoke hearts, olives, pine nuts, and basil. Cook for about 1 minute to ensure everything is heated through.
4. Serve the sauce over the pasta and sprinkle with Parmesan cheese.

Eggplant Parmesan

Eggplant Parm is an Italian favorite. The Cheesecake Factory makes a delicious version, and this recipe is inspired by that amazing dish.

Serves 2–4 | Prep. time 2 hours 15 minutes | Cooking time 10 minutes

Ingredients
1 medium Italian eggplant, peeled and cut in ½-inch slices
2 teaspoons kosher salt
½ cup all-purpose flour
1 cup eggs, beaten
2 cups Italian breadcrumbs
½ cup vegetable oil
¾ cup marinara sauce
¼ cup basil-infused olive oil
3 tablespoons Parmesan cheese, grated, divided
4 ounces mozzarella cheese, grated
⅛ teaspoon kosher salt
5 ounces angel hair pasta, cooked
½ teaspoon parsley, chopped

Directions
1. Preheat the oven to broil.
2. Line a baking sheet with paper towels. Season both sides of the eggplant circles with salt and arrange them on the pan. Cover the eggplant with another sheet of paper towel and refrigerate for 2 hours.
3. Place the flour in one bowl, the eggs in another, and the breadcrumbs in a third bowl.
4. After 2 hours, remove the eggplant from the fridge and dry the slices with fresh paper towel. One at a time, dip the slices in flour, then in the egg, and finally in the breadcrumbs. Set them aside.
5. Heat the oil in a large skillet over medium heat. Fry the eggplant for about 2 minutes on each side and set them on a plate lined with paper towel.
6. Heat the marinara sauce in a small saucepan and the basil oil in another small pan.
7. Place a wire rack in a baking dish and transfer the cooked eggplant slices to the rack. Sprinkle on 2 tablespoons of the Parmesan cheese and the mozzarella, then put the pan under the broiler until the cheese melts.
8. Serve the cooked pasta topped with eggplant. Pour some marinara over the top. Drizzle basil oil and sprinkle with the remaining Parmesan cheese and parsley.

Four Cheese Pasta

You can never go wrong with pasta covered in cheese. The Cheesecake Factory's four cheese pasta inspires this recipe of the same name.

Serves 4 | Prep. time 10 minutes | Cooking time 35 minutes

Ingredients
1 ½ cups ricotta cheese
2 ½ cups mozzarella cheese, shredded
1 egg, beaten
⅛ teaspoon black pepper
¼ cup basil leaves, sliced
8 ounces rigatoni or pasta noodles of choice (cooked and drained)
½ jar pasta sauce (such as Classico® Fire Roasted Tomato & Garlic)
½ cup Parmesan cheese, shredded

Directions
1. Preheat the oven to 350°F.
2. In a mixing bowl, mix together the ricotta, mozzarella, egg, pepper, and basil.
3. In a baking dish, combine the cooked pasta, cheese mixture, and pasta sauce. Stir to combine thoroughly. Cover with aluminum foil and bake for 25 minutes. Remove the foil and bake 5–10 minutes more, or until the cheese is bubbly.
4. Serve with shredded parmesan.

Flatbread Pizza

This recipe is inspired by the amazing Flatbread Pizza from The Cheesecake Factory. This fresh tomato pizza can be cooked on the grill or under the broiler.

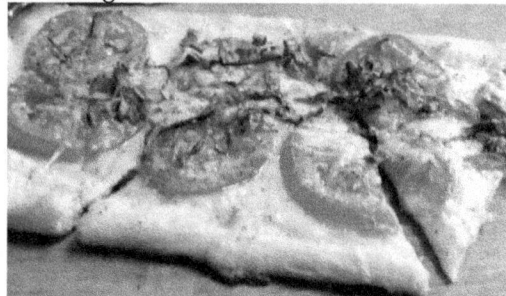

Serves 4 | Prep. time 10 minutes | Cooking time 10 minutes

Ingredients

1 (8-ounce) package cream cheese, softened
⅔ cup Parmesan cheese, grated, divided
2 tablespoons minced fresh Italian parsley, divided
1 tablespoon chives, minced
2 garlic cloves, minced
½ teaspoon fresh thyme, minced
¼ teaspoon salt
¼ teaspoon pepper
1 (14-ounce) tube refrigerated pizza crust
2 tablespoons olive oil
3 medium tomatoes, thinly sliced

Directions

1. Preheat the oven to broil.
2. In a mixing bowl, beat together the cream cheese, half the Parmesan, half the parsley, chives, garlic, thyme, salt, and pepper.
3. Roll out the pizza crust into a rectangle and arrange it on a baking sheet. Broil for about 2 minutes.
4. Top the crust with the cheese mixture and sliced tomatoes, and sprinkle on the remaining Parmesan and parsley. Return it to the oven and cook an additional 2–3 minutes, or until the cheese topping is bubbly and the crust turns a light brown.

Beef and Pork
Shepherd's Pie

This Cheesecake Factory favorite inspires the recipe for this delicious Shepherd's Pie.

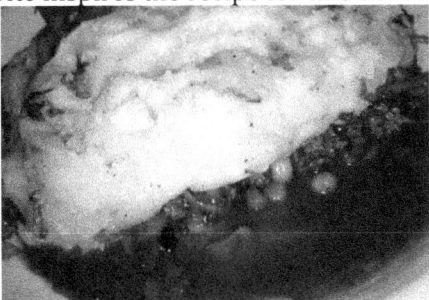

Serves 4 | Prep. time 10 minutes | Cooking time 20 minutes

Ingredients

1 pound ground beef
1 cup onion, diced
2 cups frozen corn, thawed
2 cups frozen peas, thawed
2 tablespoons ketchup
1 tablespoon Worcestershire sauce
2 teaspoons garlic, minced
1 tablespoon cornstarch
1 teaspoon beef bouillon granules
½ cup cold water
½ cup sour cream
3 ½ cups mashed potatoes (prepared with milk and butter)
¾ cup shredded cheddar cheese

Directions

1. In a large skillet, brown the ground beef and onion over medium-high heat. Drain off any excess fat.
2. Add the corn, peas, ketchup, Worcestershire sauce, and garlic. Stir well to combine, and then reduce the heat to medium low and cook for approximately 5 minutes, or until mixture the becomes bubbly.
3. Make a slurry by stirring the corn starch and bouillon into the ½ cup of water. Stir until it is smooth, then stir it into the beef mixture and cook for about 2 more minutes. Stir in the sour cream and heat through.
4. Cover the mixture with the mashed potatoes, and sprinkle on the cheese. Place the lid on the skillet and cook until the cheese melts.
5. Serve.

Meatloaf

The Cheesecake Factory has a knack for taking traditional recipes and making them better. This recipe is inspired by their delicious meatloaf.

Serves 6 | Prep. time 15 minutes | Cooking time 60 minutes

Ingredients
1 tablespoon vegetable oil
2 tablespoons green bell pepper, minced
2 tablespoons red bell pepper, minced
½ cup red onion, minced
⅓ cup carrot, shredded
5 teaspoons garlic, minced
3 eggs, beaten
1 ½ pounds ground sirloin
1 pound ground pork
1 tablespoon Italian parsley, minced

1 tablespoon granulated sugar
2 teaspoons salt
1 ½ teaspoons dried thyme
1 teaspoon ground black pepper
1 teaspoon dried oregano
1 teaspoon rubbed (ground) sage
½ teaspoon paprika
¾ cup whole milk
¾ cup bread crumbs

<u>Onion Topping</u>
2 tablespoons butter
1 medium onion, sliced

¼ teaspoon salt
¼ teaspoon ground black pepper

<u>Mushroom Gravy</u>
2 tablespoons butter
1 teaspoon garlic, minced
2 tablespoons all-purpose flour
2 cups beef broth
1 ½ cups sliced mushrooms

1 teaspoon minced Italian parsley
¼ teaspoon salt
¼ teaspoon ground black pepper
¼ teaspoon dried thyme
¼ teaspoon rubbed (ground) sage

Directions
1. Preheat the oven to 350°F.
2. Prepare the meatloaf. In a medium skillet, heat the 1 tablespoon of vegetable oil and cook the peppers and red onion until they are soft. Add the carrot and garlic and cook for 5 minutes.
3. In a large mixing bowl, beat the eggs. Add the ground beef and pork and mix them together. Add the parsley, sugar, salt, thyme, pepper, oregano, sage, paprika, the cooked vegetables, and the milk. Once this is combined, add the breadcrumbs a bit at a time so they get evenly distributed.
4. Press the meat mixture into a loaf pan and bake for 60 minutes. After 60 minutes, remove loaf from oven and let stand for 30 more minutes.
5. Make the onion topping and gravy while the meatloaf is cooking.
6. To make the onion topping, melt 2 tablespoons of butter in a medium skillet, then add the onion, salt, and pepper and cook for about 25 minutes. Keep the heat relatively low to caramelize the onion without burning it.
7. Make the gravy by melting the butter in a small saucepan. Add the garlic and cook until fragrant, then whisk in the flour. Cook until the flour starts to brown, about 3 minutes.
8. Whisk in the beef broth and make sure there are no lumps. Then add the mushrooms, parsley, salt, pepper, thyme, and sage. Cook until the gravy thickens, about 10–12 minutes.
9. Serve sliced meatloaf topped with onions and gravy.

Steak Diane

Another Cheesecake Factory favorite inspires this amazingly delicious recipe you can make at home.

Serves 2 | Prep. time 10 minutes | Cooking time 15 minutes

Ingredients
2–3 tablespoons butter
12 ounces beef tenderloin, cut into 3-ounce medallions
Salt to taste
2 teaspoons cracked whole black peppercorns
½ cup fresh mushrooms, sliced
3 tablespoons pearl onions, chopped
¼ cup brandy or white wine
1 teaspoon Worcestershire sauce
1 tablespoon Dijon mustard
¾ cup beef stock
¼ cup cream

Directions
1. Preheat the oven to 350°F.
2. In a large skillet, melt 2 tablespoons of the butter over medium-high heat.
3. Sprinkle both sides of the beef medallions with salt and fresh pepper. Sear them for about 2 minutes on each side, and then remove them from the skillet to an ovenproof dish and transfer it to the oven to keep warm.
4. While those are in the oven, add a bit more butter to the skillet. Add the mushrooms and pearl onions and cook until they start to turn soft. Add the white wine and Worcestershire, then stir in the mustard. Cook for about 2 minutes.
5. Stir in the beef stock and bring it to a boil. When it boils, remove it from the heat and stir in the cream.
6. Remove the beef from the oven and plate it with sauce over the top.

Pasta Carbonara

Pasta with bacon makes this Cheesecake Factory inspired dish sing with flavor.

Serves 4 | Prep. time 5 minutes | Cooking time 20 minutes

Ingredients
4 slices bacon
2 tablespoons butter
2 cloves garlic, minced
2 tablespoons all-purpose flour
¼ cup Parmesan cheese, grated, plus more for serving
1 (12-ounce) can low-fat evaporated milk
1 cup frozen peas, thawed
8 ounces spaghetti, cooked
½ –1 cup hot chicken broth or pasta water, as needed
Salt and coarsely ground black pepper to taste
2 tablespoons fresh Italian parsley, snipped

Directions
1. In a medium skillet, cook the bacon until it is crispy. Let it cool, and then break it into bite-sized pieces.
2. In a large saucepan, melt the butter and add the garlic. Cook until it is fragrant and whisk in the flour and Parmesan cheese. Cook about 2 minutes.
3. Next, a little at a time, whisk in the evaporated milk. Bring this to a boil, then reduce the heat and cook until it thickens. Stir in the peas.
4. Put the cooked spaghetti in a large bowl and add half a cup of either chicken broth or pasta water, and then stir in the sauce. If the sauce is too thick you can thin it with more water or broth.
5. Stir in the bacon pieces and serve with grated Parmesan and salt and pepper to taste. Sprinkle with parsley.

Grilled Steak Medallions

This recipe pays homage to the Cheesecake Factory's popular Steak Medallions.

Serves 8 | Prep. time 10 minutes | Cooking time 35 minutes

Ingredients
1 pound sirloin steak, cut into medallions or individual pieces
Salt and pepper to taste
1 tablespoon extra-virgin olive oil
3 tablespoons unsalted butter
3 cups mushrooms, sliced
1 medium-large shallot, minced
1 tablespoon garlic, minced
10 asparagus spears, chopped at an angle
1 cup grape tomatoes, halved
2 tablespoons flour
½ cup red wine
½ cup low-sodium beef broth
¼ teaspoon dried thyme, or one sprig of fresh thyme
1 bay leaf

Directions
1. Season the meat with salt and pepper.
2. In a large skillet, heat the olive oil until it is hot. Add the steaks and cook for 4 minutes on the first side without moving them. After 4 minutes, flip and cook an additional 2 minutes. Remove the steaks from the skillet and cover with foil to keep them warm.
3. Add 3 tablespoons of butter to the skillet. After it melts, add the mushrooms, shallots, garlic, and asparagus. Let them cook for 2–3 minutes, then stir and continue cooking until the asparagus starts to get soft. Add the grape tomatoes to heat them through.
4. Add the flour and stir to combine, and then whisk in the red wine, beef broth, thyme, and bay leaf. Bring to a boil and cook until it starts to thicken. Remove the bay leaf before serving.
5. Serve steak medallions with sauce and vegetables on top.

Cuban Sandwich

The Cheesecake Factory's lunches are as good as their dinners. This recipe is inspired by the Cheesecake Factory's Cuban sandwich.

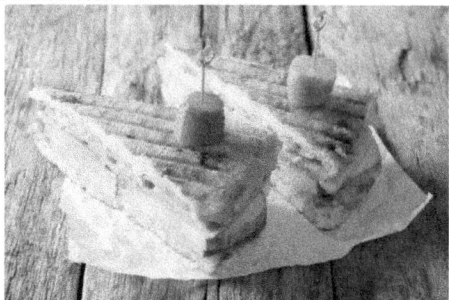

Serves 4 | Prep. time 20 minutes | Cooking time 5 minutes

Ingredients
½ teaspoon olive oil
2 garlic cloves, minced
½ cup reduced-fat mayonnaise
8 slices artisan bread
8 thick slices deli smoked turkey
4 slices deli ham
8 slices Swiss cheese
12 dill pickle slices
1 cup fresh baby spinach

Directions
1. Heat the olive oil in a small skillet. Add the garlic and cook until the garlic is fragrant. Remove it from the heat and let it cool, then stir it into the mayonnaise.
2. Spread some garlic mayo over each slice of bread, and assemble the sandwiches using turkey, ham, cheese, pickles, and spinach.
3. Cook the sandwiches in a panini maker or grill them in skillet until the cheese melts and the bread has browned up.
4. Serve.

Desserts
Pumpkin Cheesecake

This is one of the Cheesecake Factory's most popular desserts. Now you can make this recipe (inspired by the Cheesecake Factory's) at home.

Serves 8-10 | Prep. time 30 minutes plus 8 hours refrigeration time | Cooking time 1 hour 45 minutes

Ingredients

- 2 ½ cups graham cracker crumbs
- ¾ cup unsalted butter, melted
- 2 ¾ cups granulated sugar, divided
- 1 teaspoon salt, plus a pinch
- 4 (8-ounce) blocks cream cheese, at room temperature
- ¼ cup sour cream
- 1 (15-ounce) can pure pumpkin
- 6 large eggs, room temperature
- 1 tablespoon vanilla extract
- 2 ½ teaspoons ground cinnamon
- 1 teaspoon ginger, ground
- ¼ teaspoon cloves, ground
- 2 cups whipped cream, sweetened
- ⅓ cup toasted pecans, roughly chopped

Directions

1. Preheat the oven to 325°F and grease a 12-inch springform pan.
2. In a mixing bowl, combine the graham cracker crumbs, melted butter, ¼ cup of the sugar, and a pinch of salt. Mix until well combined and press the mixture into the prepared springform pan. Bake for about 25 minutes.
3. While the crust is baking, begin making the filling by beating together the cream cheese, sour cream, and pumpkin.
4. Add the rest of the sugar, and slowly incorporate the beaten eggs and vanilla. Add the remaining salt, cinnamon, ginger, and cloves.
5. Fill a large baking pan (big enough to hold your springform pan) with about half an inch of water. Place it in the oven and let the water get hot.
6. Put foil around the edges of your springform pan, then add the filling and place the pan in the oven inside the water bath you made with the baking pan.
7. Bake for 1 hour and 45 minutes, or until the center is set. You can turn the foil over the edges of the cake if it starts to get too brown. Remove the pan from the oven and place it on a cooling rack for at least one hour before removing the sides of the springform pan.
8. After it has cooled, remove sides of the pan and refrigerate the cheesecake for at least 8 hours or overnight.
9. Serve with whipped cream and toasted pecans.

Reese's Peanut Butter Chocolate Cake Cheesecake

This is one of the Cheesecake Factory's most popular and decadent cheesecakes. This recipe is inspired by their amazing Peanut Butter Chocolate Cake Cheesecake.

Serves 8-10 | Prep. time 2 hours plus 6 hours refrigeration time | Cooking time 1 hour 15 minutes

Ingredients

Cheesecake
4 (8-ounce) packages cream cheese, softened
1 ¼ cups sugar
½ cup sour cream
2 teaspoons vanilla extract
5 eggs
8 Chocolate Peanut Butter cups, chopped
1 (14-ounce) can dulce de leche

Chocolate Cake
1 ¾ cups all-purpose flour
2 cups sugar
¾ cup cocoa
2 teaspoons baking soda
1 teaspoon salt
2 eggs, room temp
1 cup buttermilk
½ cup butter, melted
1 tablespoon vanilla extract
1 cup black coffee, hot

Peanut Butter Buttercream
¾ cup butter
¾ cup shortening
¾ cup peanut butter
1 ½ teaspoons vanilla
4-5 cups powdered sugar

Ganache
2 cups semi-sweet chocolate chips
1 cup heavy cream
1 teaspoon vanilla

Directions

1.   Preheat the oven to 350°F and grease a 9-inch springform pan.
2.   Make the cheesecake. Preheat the oven to 475°F. Fill a large baking pan (your springform pan with have to fit in it) with half an inch of water and place it in the oven while it preheats.
3.   Beat the cream cheese in a large bowl until it is fluffy. Gradually incorporate the sugar, sour cream, and vanilla, and mix well.

4. Add the eggs one at a time and beat until just combined. Fold in the peanut butter cups and pour the batter into the springform pan. Bake at 475°F for 15 minutes, then reduce the heat to 350°F and bake for 60 minutes, or until the center is completely set.
5. Remove the cake from the oven and let it cool for 60 minutes before taking off the sides of the springform pan. When it is completely cool, refrigerate the cheesecake for at least 6 hours, but 8 hours to overnight would be better. When it is completely cold, cut the cheesecake in half to make two layers.
6. Meanwhile, make the chocolate cake: mix the flour, sugar, cocoa, baking soda, and salt together in a large bowl. Mix in the eggs, buttermilk, melted butter, and vanilla, and beat until it is smooth. Slowly incorporate the coffee.
7. Grease and flour two 9-inch round cake pans. Pour the batter evenly into each pan and bake for 30–35 minutes. When fully cooked, remove the cakes from the oven and cool for 15 minutes before taking them out of the pans. When fully cooled, wrap each cake in plastic wrap and refrigerate until ready to assemble the cake.
8. Make the buttercream frosting by beating together the butter and shortening, then add the peanut butter and vanilla. Mix in the powdered sugar one cup at a time until you achieve the desired sweetness and consistency.
9. To assemble, put one layer of chocolate cake on a cake plate. Drizzle half of the dulce de leche over the top of the cake. Top that with a layer of cheesecake, and spread peanut butter frosting over the top of the cheesecake. Repeat to make a second layer. When assembled, place the whole cake in the freezer for about an hour to fully set.
10. Make the ganache by melting chocolate chips with heavy cream and vanilla in a small saucepan. When the cake is completely set, pour ganache over the top. Refrigerate until ganache the sets.

White Chocolate Raspberry Swirl Cheesecake

This White Chocolate Raspberry Swirl Cheesecake is one of the Cheesecake Factory's most popular desserts. This recipe is inspired by that luscious creamy cake.

Serves 8-10 | Prep. time 45 minutes plus 5 hours refrigeration | Cooking time 1 hour 15 minutes

Ingredients

Crust
1 ½ cups chocolate cookie crumbs, such as crumbled Oreo® cookies
⅓ cup butter, melted

Filling
4 (8-ounce) packages cream cheese
1 ¼ cups granulated sugar
½ cup sour cream
2 teaspoons vanilla extract
½ cup raspberry preserves (or raspberry pie filling)
¼ cup water
5 eggs
4 ounces white chocolate, chopped into chunks

Optional Garnish
2 ounces shaved white chocolate (optional)
Fresh whipped cream

Directions

1. Preheat the oven to 475°F.
2. In a food processor, crumble the cookies and add the melted butter. Press the mixture into a greased 9-inch springform pan, and place in the freezer while you make the filling.
3. Pour half an inch of water in a large baking pan (it needs to fit your springform pan) and place it in the oven.
4. In a mixing bowl, beat together the cream cheese, sugar, sour cream, and vanilla. Scrape the sides of the bowl after the ingredients have been well combined.
5. Beat the eggs in a small bowl then add them slowly to the cream cheese mixture.
6. In another small dish, mix the raspberry preserves and water. Microwave for 1 minute. If you want to remove the raspberry seeds you can run the hot liquid through a mesh strainer.
7. Remove the crust from the freezer and cover the outside bottom of the pan with aluminum foil. Sprinkle the white chocolate over the crust, then pour half of the cheesecake batter into the springform pan. Next, drizzle half of the raspberry preserves over the top of the batter. Then add the rest of the batter with the rest of the drizzle.
8. Place the springform pan into the water bath and bake for 15 minutes at 475°F, then reduce the heat to 350°F and bake about 60 more minutes more, or until the center of the cake is set and cake is cooked through.
9. Remove from oven and cool it completely before removing sides of pan, then move to the refrigerator for at least 5 hours.
10. Serve with extra white chocolate and fresh whipped cream.

Carrot Cake Cheesecake

What do you get when you combine carrot cake with cheesecake? This delicious recipe that is inspired by the Cheesecake Factory's favorite.

Serves 12 | Prep. time 20 minutes plus 5 hours refrigeration time | Cooking time 50–60 minutes

Ingredients

Cheesecake
- 2 (8-ounce) blocks cream cheese, at room temperature
- ¾ cup granulated sugar
- 1 tablespoon flour
- 3 eggs
- 1 teaspoon vanilla

Carrot Cake
- ¾ cup vegetable oil
- 1 cup granulated sugar
- 2 eggs
- 1 teaspoon vanilla
- 1 cup flour
- 1 teaspoon baking soda
- 1 teaspoon cinnamon
- 1 dash salt
- 1 (8-ounce) can crushed pineapple, well drained with juice reserved
- 1 cup grated carrot
- ½ cup flaked coconut
- ½ cup chopped walnuts

Pineapple Cream Cheese Frosting
- 2 ounces cream cheese, softened
- 1 tablespoon butter, softened
- 1 ¾ cups powdered sugar
- ½ teaspoon vanilla
- 1 tablespoon reserved pineapple juice

Directions

1. Preheat the oven to 350°F and grease a 9-inch springform pan.
2. In a large bowl, beat together the cream cheese and the sugar until smooth. Then beat in the flour, eggs, and vanilla until well combined. Set aside.
3. In another large bowl, beat together the ¾ cup vegetable oil, sugar, eggs and vanilla until smooth. Then add the flour, baking soda, cinnamon and salt and beat until smooth. Fold in the crushed pineapple, grated carrot, coconut, and walnuts.
4. Pour 1 ½ cups of the carrot cake batter into the prepared pan. Drop large spoonfuls of the cream cheese batter over the top of the carrot cake batter. Then add spoonfuls of carrot cake batter over the top of the cream cheese batter. Repeat with the remaining batter.
5. Bake the cake for 50–60 minutes, or until the center is set. Remove it from the oven and cool for about an hour before taking the sides off the springform pan. Refrigerate for at least 5 hours.
6. While the cake is cooling, make the frosting. Beating together all the frosting ingredients. Frost the cake when it is completely cold.

Original Cheesecake

No matter how many versions of cheesecakes the famous restaurant invents, the original cheesecake will always have a special place in our hearts—and now in our recipe lists.

Serves: 12 – Preparation Time: 4 hours 15 minutes – Cooking Time: 1 hour 5 minutes

Ingredients

Crust:
1 ½ cups graham cracker crumbs
¼ teaspoon ground cinnamon
⅓ cup margarine, melted

Filling:
4 (8-ounce) packages cream cheese, softened
1 ¼ cups white sugar
½ cup sour cream
2 teaspoons vanilla extract
5 large eggs

Topping:
½ cup sour cream
2 teaspoons sugar

Preparation

1. Preheat the oven to 475°F and place a skillet with half an inch of water inside.
2. Combine the ingredients for the crust in a bowl. Line a large pie pan with parchment paper, and spread crust onto pan. Press firmly. Cover it with foil, and keep it in the freezer until ready to use.
3. Combine all the ingredients for the filling EXCEPT the eggs in a bowl. Scrape the sides of the bowl while beating, until mixture is smooth. Mix in eggs one at a time, and beat until fully blended.
4. Take the crust from the freezer and pour in the filling, spreading it evenly. Place the pie pan into the heated skillet in the oven, and bake for about 12 minutes.
5. Reduce the heat to 350°F. Continue to bake for about 50 minutes, or until the top of the cake is golden. Remove it from the oven and transfer the skillet onto a wire rack to cool.
6. Prepare the topping by mixing all ingredients in a bowl. Coat the cake with the topping, then cover. Refrigerate for at least 4 hours.
7. Serve cold.

Ultimate Red Velvet Cheesecake

This may take a little more time and effort compared to other dishes and desserts, but I promise it will all be worth it once you take that first gloriously perfect bite.

Serves: 16 – Preparation Time: 3 hours 30 minutes – Cooking Time: 1 hour 15 minutes

Ingredients
Cheesecake:
2 (8-ounce) packages cream cheese, softened
⅔ cup granulated white sugar
Pinch salt
2 large eggs
⅓ cup sour cream
⅓ cup heavy whipping cream
1 teaspoon vanilla extract
Non-stick cooking spray
Hot water, for water bath

Red velvet cake:
2 ½ cups all-purpose flour
1 ½ cups granulated white sugar
3 tablespoons unsweetened cocoa powder
1 ½ teaspoons baking soda
1 teaspoon salt
2 large eggs
1 ½ cups vegetable oil
1 cup buttermilk
¼ cup red food coloring
2 teaspoons vanilla extract
2 teaspoons white vinegar

Frosting:
2 ½ cups powdered sugar, sifted
2 (8-ounce) packages cream cheese, softened
½ cup unsalted butter, softened
1 tablespoon vanilla extract

Preparation
1. For the cheesecake, preheat the oven to 325°F.
2. Beat the cream cheese, sugar, and salt for about 2 minutes, until creamy and smooth. Add the eggs, mixing again after adding each one. Add the sour cream, heavy cream, and vanilla extract, and beat until smooth and well blended.
3. Coat a springform pan with non-stick cooking spray, then place parchment paper on top. Wrap the outsides entirely with two layers of aluminum foil. (This is to prevent water from the water bath from entering the pan.)

4. Pour the cream cheese batter into the pan, then place it in a roasting pan. Add boiling water to the roasting pan to surround the springform pan. Place it in the oven and bake for 45 minutes, until set.
5. Transfer the springform pan with the cheesecake onto a rack to cool for about 1 hour. Refrigerate overnight.
6. For the red velvet cake, preheat the oven to 350°F.
7. Combine the flour, sugar, cocoa powder, baking soda, and salt in a large bowl.
8. In a separate bowl, mix the eggs, oil, buttermilk, food coloring, vanilla and vinegar. Add the wet ingredients to dry ingredients. Blend for 1 minute with a mixer on medium-low speed, then on high speed for 2 minutes.
9. Spray non-stick cooking spray in 2 metal baking pans that are the same size as the springform pan used for the cheesecake. Coat the bottoms thinly with flour. Divide the batter between them.
10. Bake for about 30–35 minutes. The cake is done when only a few crumbs attach to a toothpick when inserted in the center. Transfer the cakes to a rack and let them cool for 10 minutes. Separate the cakes from the pans using a knife around the edges, then invert them onto the rack. Let them cool completely.
11. To prepare the frosting, mix the powdered sugar, cream cheese, butter, and vanilla using a mixer on medium-high speed, just until smooth.
12. Assemble the cake by positioning one red velvet cake layer onto a cake plate. Remove the cheesecake from the pan, peel off the parchment paper, and layer it on top of the red velvet cake layer. Top with the second red velvet cake layer.
13. Coat a thin layer of prepared frosting on the entire outside of the cake. Clean the spatula every time you scoop out from bowl of frosting, so as to not mix crumbs into it. Refrigerate for 30 minutes to set. Then coat cake the with a second layer by adding a large scoop on top then spreading it to the top side of the cake then around it.
14. Cut into slices. Serve.

Strawberry Shortcake

Strawberry shortcake is almost as American as apple pie. This recipe is a version of the Cheesecake Factory favorite you can make at home.

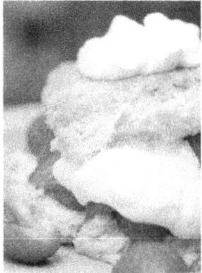

Yields 16 bars | Prep. time 5 minutes | Cooking time 2 hours and 15 minutes

Ingredients

Sugared Strawberries:
2 cups strawberries (sliced)
¼ cup granulated sugar

Whipped Cream:
4 cups heavy cream
½ cup powdered sugar
¼ teaspoon vanilla

Shortcake Biscuit:
4 ½ cups all-purpose flour
½ cup sugar
5 tablespoons baking powder
2 teaspoons salt
1 ¾ cups butter
2 cups heavy cream
2 cups buttermilk
2 scoops vanilla ice cream

Directions

1. Preheat the oven to 375°F.
2. In a bowl, combine the sliced strawberries with the sugar. Stir, cover, and refrigerate for 2 hours.
3. Chill a mixing bowl and beat the heavy cream, powdered sugar, and vanilla until soft peaks form. Don't over beat or you will lose the fluffy consistency. Refrigerate.
4. In a mixing bowl, mix together the flour, sugar, baking powder, and salt. Stir to combine. Using two butter knives, cut the butter into the flour mixture until it becomes crumbly. Add the cream and the buttermilk and mix gently until the batter forms.
5. Turn out the dough onto a floured surface, and roll it to form biscuits about half an inch thick. Take care not to turn the cutter as you remove it from the dough.
6. Place the biscuits on a non-stick cookie sheet and bake for about 15 minutes. They should at least double in size.
7. When they cool, assemble the shortcake by cutting each biscuit in half, topping the bottom half with strawberries and ice cream, and placing the top half of the biscuit on top of the ice cream. Top with more strawberries and whipped cream.

Lemoncello Cream Torte

Filling, and beautiful, this budget-friendly recipe can be served as dessert or even as a delicious breakfast.

Serves 8-10 | Prep. time 15 minutes | Refrigeration time 4-5 hours

Ingredients
1 box yellow cake mix
Limoncello liqueur (optional)
1 package ladyfinger cookies
1 (3-ounce) package sugar-free lemon gelatin
1 cup boiling water
1 (8-ounce) package cream cheese, softened
1 teaspoon vanilla extract
1 (13-ounce) can cold milnot (evaporated milk), whipped

For the glaze:
1 cup confectioner's sugar
1–2 tablespoons lemon juice

Directions
1. Preheat the oven to 350°F.
2. Prepare the yellow cake mix according to the directions on the package. Use two 9-inch round cake pans, or you can use a springform pan and cut the cake in half after it is baked.
3. When the cake is done and cooled, you can soak the layers lightly with some limoncello. Do the same with the ladyfingers.
4. Bring one cup of water to a boil and stir in the lemon gelatin. Refrigerate until it gets thick, but don't let it set.
5. Mix together the cream cheese and vanilla, then mix in the thickened gelatin. Fold the whipped milnot into the mixture until combined.
6. To assemble the cake, place the bottom layer of the cake back in the pan. This will help you get even layers. Top the cake with about half an inch of the lemon filling. Place ladyfingers on top of the filling, then top with another layer of the filling. Place the other half of the cake on the top.
7. Place the cake in the refrigerator to set.
8. Make a drizzle with some lemon juice and confectioner's sugar, and drizzle over the cake.

Oreo Cookie Cheesecake

Everyone loves Oreos® and this recipe is a tribute to the Cheesecake Factory's version of Oreo Cookie Cheesecake we all love.

Serves 8–10| Prep. time 10 minutes plus 4–6 hours refrigeration time | Cooking Time 60 minutes

Ingredients
1 package Oreo cookies
⅓ cup unsalted butter, melted
3 (8-ounce) packages cream cheese
¾ cup granulated sugar
4 eggs
1 cup sour cream
1 teaspoon vanilla extract
Whipped cream and additional cookies for garnish

Directions
1. Preheat the oven to 350°F.
2. Crush most of the cookies (25-30) in a food processor or blender, and add the melted butter. Press the cookie mixture into the bottom of a 9-inch springform pan and keep it in the refrigerator while you prepare the filling.
3. In a mixing bowl, beat the cream cheese until smooth, and add the sugar. Beat in the eggs in one a time. When the eggs are mixed together, beat in the sour cream and vanilla.
4. Chop the remaining cookies and fold them gently into the filling mixture.
5. Pour the filling into the springform pan and bake at 350°F for 50–60 minutes. Ensure the center of the cake has set.
6. Let the cake cool for 15 minutes, then carefully remove the sides of the springform pan. Transfer to the refrigerator and refrigerate for 4–6 hours or overnight.

Banana Cream Cheesecake

The Cheesecake Factory is obviously famous for its cheesecakes. This make-at-home version of the restaurant favorite will surely impress.

Serves 4 | Prep. time 20 minutes | Cooking time 1 hour 30 minutes

Ingredients
20 vanilla sandwich cookies
¼ cup margarine, melted
3 (8-ounce) packages cream cheese, softened
⅔ cup granulated sugar
2 tablespoons cornstarch
3 eggs
¾ cup mashed bananas
½ cup whipping cream
2 teaspoons vanilla extract

Directions
1. Preheat the oven to 350°F.
2. Crush the cookies in either a food processor or blender. When they have turned to crumbs, add the melted butter. Place the mixture in a springform pan and press to entirely cover the bottom and up the sides of the pan. Refrigerate this while you prepare the filling.
3. Beat the cream cheese until it is smooth, and add the sugar and corn starch. When the cheese mixture is well blended, add in the eggs one at a time.
4. When the eggs are incorporated, add the bananas, whipping cream, and vanilla, beating until well combined.
5. Pour the filling into the springform pan and bake at 350°F for 15 minutes. Reduce the heat to 200°F and bake until the center of the cheesecake is set, about 1 hour and 15 minutes.
6. When the center is set, remove the cake from the oven. Pop the spring on the pan, but don't remove the sides until the cheesecake has cooled completely. When it is cool, transfer it to the refrigerator. Refrigerate for at least 4 hours before serving.
7. Serve with whipped cream and freshly sliced bananas.

Blackout Cake

Not every delicious dessert has to be cheesecake! This decadent chocolate cake will satisfy those chocolate cravings. This recipe is said to be as close as you can get to recreating the restaurant favorite. To make the original, you will need an 8-inch pastry/cake ring. But it's not necessary, 3 cake 8-inch cake pan will work as well.

Serves 8–10 | Prep. time 30 minutes | Cook time 35–45 minutes

Ingredients
For the Cake:
1 cup butter, softened
4 cups sugar
4 large eggs
4 teaspoons vanilla extract, divided
6 ounces unsweetened chocolate, melted
For the Chocolate Ganache:
12 ounces semisweet chocolate, chips or chopped
3 cups heavy cream
4 tablespoons butter, chopped

4 cups flour
4 teaspoons baking soda
½ teaspoon salt
1 cup buttermilk
1 ¾ cups boiling water

2 teaspoons vanilla
1 ½ cups roasted almonds, crushed (for garnish)

Directions
1. Preheat the oven to 350°F. Prepare two large rimmed baking sheets with parchment paper (or grease and dust with flour 3 8-inch cake pans).
2. In a large bowl or bowl for a stand mixer, beat together the butter and sugar until well combined. When the sugar mixture is fluffy, add the eggs and 2 teaspoons of vanilla. When that is combined, add the 4 ounces of melted chocolate and mix well.
3. In a separate bowl, stir together the flour, baking soda, and salt. Gradually add half the flour mixture to the chocolate mixture. When it is combined, add half of the buttermilk and mix until combined. Repeat with remaining flour mixture and buttermilk. When it is completely combined, add the boiling water and mix thoroughly. (The batter should be a little thin).
4. Divide the batter evenly between the two large baking sheets that you prepared earlier (or 3 8-inch cake pans).
5. Transfer to the oven and bake for 20–30 minutes for the baking sheets or 25-35 minutes for the cake pans, or until a toothpick inserted in the center comes out clean.
6. Remove from the oven and let cakes cool for about 10 minutes. With the pastry ring, make 3 cakes from each of the baking sheet. When they are completely cool down. If using cake pans, turn them out onto a cooling rack and let them cool completely and then cut horizontally into two to make 6 cake layers.
7. Make the ganache by mixing the chocolate chips and cream in a heat-safe glass bowl. Place the bowl over a pot of boiling water. Reduce heat to medium-low and let simmer gently. Stir constantly with a wooden spoon until the chocolate is all melted. Add-in the butter and vanilla and stir until well combined. Let cool for a few minutes, cover with plastic wrap, and refrigerate until the ganache holds its shape and is spreadable, about 10 minutes.
8. To assemble the cake, place the first cake layer on a serving plate and spread a some of the ganache on the top. Place second cake layer on top and spread some of the ganache on top. Repeat until all 6 layers are done. Use the remaining ganache to frost the top and sides of the cake, then cover the sides with crushed almonds (if desired) by pressing them gently into the chocolate ganache. Refrigerate before serving.